This Old Dog

An owner's guide to providing the best care for your senior dog.

SHAUNA SLOBODIAN

Disclaimer

The content of this book is for educational purposes only. It is not intended to diagnose, treat or prevent any condition or disease. You understand that this book is not intended as a substitute for consultation with a veterinarian. Please consult with your own veterinarian or canine rehab therapist regarding the suggestions and recommendations made in this book. The use of this book implies your acceptance of this disclaimer.

Dedication

To my mom Vicky. She brought home my first dog when I was 10. She had no idea the impact it would have on my life or my future career path. She did so many things for Bubbles that truly showed what the love for a dog is. Bubbles, our beloved yellow Labrador retriever, lived until 16.5 years old. That old dog and my *young* mom are the inspiration for writing this book. Thank you, mom, for all the support and guidance you have provided me over the years. I love you.

Me, my brother Donovan, my mom and that "old dog" Bubbles in 1997.

Foreword

For years now, I have come to believe that domesticated animals, and dogs in particular, are angels on earth. Here to teach us lessons about life and provide us with opportunities to learn and grow. They help us to navigate through the many different stages and experiences in our own lives, and as they age, they require us to help them to navigate through that stage of their life.

This Old Dog is a book that helps you to fulfil a promise. A promise you may not have known you made. A promise you made when you brought a dog into your life. A promise you made to do right by your dog, right to the end. There is so much to treasure in an old dog. So much to love. So much to admire. There is also so much you can do to help them at this stage in their life to have the best life they can possibly have.

I commend Shauna for writing this book. It is written in such a way that the information is accessible to all. It thoughtfully explains concepts and suggestions and is organized in a logical fashion to take you down the road of potential senior dog problems to practical solutions. It answers questions. It provides hope. It gives you tools to help your old dog thrive in its old age.

Kudos must also go to you, the reader, in adding this book to your library and knowledge base. There are 'people who own dogs' and then there are 'dog people'. If you are reading this book, you know which you are, and you're in good company here!

Wishing you all many more happy, healthy, loving, and cherished years with your old dog.

Laurie Edge-Hughes, BScPT, MAnimSt (Animal Physiotherapy), CAFCI, CCRT

Owner, Four Leg Rehab Inc.

Co-Owner, The Canine Fitness Centre Ltd.

Acknowledgements

There are a few people that deserve my thanks for this book finally being finished.

First is Jeremy Sutton, aka "the book boss". He gave me the tools, confidence and constant reminders to get this thing done! Who dat!

Secondly, thank you to Lorna Clarke and Maha Najd for taking the time to review this book and give me edits and feedback. Your thoughts were invaluable. I'm blessed to call you both friends.

Lastly, thank you to my husband Dave for never doubting I could write this book, being my own personal cheerleader, reading this book countless times for editing and being my photographer for the exercise section! I love you.

Thank you to everyone who contributed their photos to help bring this book to life:

Laurie Edge-Hughes	Kelly Ladouceur
Amy Desourdy-Carter	Margaret Pearson Krealing
Alexis Kelly Bond	Pam Wigger
April Devitt	Kimberly Ranae Lanus-Saice
Jen Hanks	Rosemary Hegarty
Maha Najd	Mikii Savvage
Tania Rudkin Roth	Amelia Chambers
Anic Belgiorno	Edriana Fermin
Allison Smith	Kathy Therens
Daryl Bell	Carolyn McIntyre
Tracy Patterson Allshouse	Jenny Moe
Cynthia Thompson	Amanda Gilbert

Table of Contents

Introduction

Why write another book on senior dog care when there are plenty out there already? Good question. It would have been easy enough to point friends, family, clients and colleagues to the many resources out there that exist already and tell them to use any one of those. But that wasn't enough for me.

I've spent a decade working with senior humans and have decided to focus my canine practice on working with senior dogs as well. I think there is something special about the experiences and life spent of a senior whether human or canine. They have wisdom in their years but I have found they are often overlooked and sometimes brushed off by their healthcare providers. I saw it for years with people and now see the same with dogs. Owners are often leaving vet appointments with the feeling that they were just told "well, he/she is old and you will have to deal with it" and without any sound, practical advice about what they can actually do to help their dog.

The purpose of this book was not to cover every ailment that a senior dog could ever experience. I don't have the expertise to do that, nor would it provide an owner with tangible, easy to digest things that they can actually do to help their dog. I've tried to approach this book using my background as a physiotherapist and also as a dog owner. I thought about what I am often talking to owners about and what I would want to know about caring for my own senior dog. Often there can be some relief in knowing what are common issues and just having a few things to try in order to manage the situation better.

What do I hope that you get from this book? First and foremost, I hope that it is an easy-to-read reference for owners of senior dogs. I have tried to be clear in different areas of the book where it is my best advice to refer you back to your vet for more help. I hope that it gives you some food for thought about how you can make small changes in your day-to-day routine that may help both you and your dog. Lastly, I hope you find it an enjoyable read that reaffirms your love, commitment and devotion to your old dog.

1

Me and my crazy yellow lab Maggie Mae.

~ 1 ~

The Joys of a Senior Dog

You've reached the golden years with your dog. They are firmly an established member of the family and they have been for many years. You have lots of memories with your dog from over the years - the day you brought them home, how they reacted to the birth of a child, funny things they did that made you laugh.

You are past the sometimes-obnoxious puppy phase and your sweet dog has probably settled into a predictable routine that you dare not change or they will let you know you've screwed up! No longer do you have to worry about leaving them unattended with your running shoes. You've been through the training and you are long into reaping the rewards of your hard work in those early months.

A senior dog is usually calm and grateful. Don't they just seem so much more pleased with your praise or a treat than when they were younger? And they are often up for a good snuggle and are happy to just spend some quiet time with you. Sometimes the best moments are those quiet moments.

And there is something sweet and sacred about the joyful face of a senior dog. You can see wisdom and knowledge in their salt and peppered faces. Their eyes draw you in and you can't help but smile when they realize you are looking right back at them and they start to wag their tail.

It can also be a time of bracing for heartache. Your dog may be starting to slow down or show their age and you worry. Worry about doing what's right for them so they live a long life. Worry about them being in pain. Worry about knowing when it might be time to say goodbye.

The chapters ahead are written to educate you, the senior dog owner, so that you have the confidence to do what is right for your dog and to keep them as a healthy, active, loyal member of your family for as long as possible.

Freya at age 13.

~ 2 ~

When is your Dog a Senior?

There is no set age at which a dog officially becomes a senior. It is different for small dogs and large dogs. Smaller dogs like chihuahuas, may not be a senior until they are over 10 years old. Large and giant breed dogs, like a Great Dane, might be considered a senior sooner at only 5 years old. The old adage that every dog year is equivalent to 7 human years doesn't hold up either. One dog year is more human years for a large dog than a small dog who generally has a longer life span. It has been suggested that dogs spend the last quarter of their lives as seniors. But then again, we won't know what years those senior ones were until they are gone.

Greying or white hair on a dog is not a good indicator either. Some dogs may experience these changes at only a year old but their attitude and playfulness doesn't change.

Maybe we would be better suited to look for *signs of aging* instead of concerning ourselves about whether they are an adult or a senior. Signs of aging might include:

Decreasing tolerance for exercise or activity. Is your dog having difficulty keeping up on the same length of walk they used to do without any problem? Or, do you find that your playtime in the backyard tires them out more than it used to? There can be many reasons for your dog slowing down including arthritis pain and decreased muscle mass.

Lipomas. Lipomas are usually benign tumours often found on the underside of the dog though they can grow anywhere. They are fat-filled sacs that are increasingly common as a dog ages but pose no threat. They should be easily movable and well defined. They don't need to be removed unless they start to affect your dog's mobility or your dog starts to chew at them. It is best to be aware of these bumps and have them examined by your vet on the off-chance that it could be something more serious.

Age-related conditions. Just like humans, dogs experience arthritis. It is a common part of aging but there are many things that can be done to help slow down and manage the symptoms of arthritis. Chapter 5 covers arthritis in much more detail. Incontinence, weakness, cancers and vestibular disease are also more common with age and are covered in chapter 6.

Behaviour changes. Changes in your dog's behaviour may be a sign of pain or of your dog not feeling well. If your dog seems to be experiencing confusion or memory loss it may be a sign of canine cognitive dysfunction. Look for more in chapter 7.

Weight loss or gain. Weight gain may be caused by decreasing levels of activity. Weight loss, on the other hand, can be caused by a decreased drive to eat. Both are concerning and need to be addressed. Chapter 8 will cover this.

Loss of senses (vision and hearing). Just like humans, a dog's senses can decline as they age. Rest assured they often cope much better than humans.

Angel lost her sight due to a tumor at age 11 but adapted quickly.

~ 3 ~

What is Normal for your Dog

Knowing what is normal for your dog can be a great way to be able to identify problems when they arise. Often, we go through our normal day-to-day lives without giving much consideration for what we are doing. If we were to step back and reflect on what we are doing with our dogs, how they are moving and what their normal behaviours are, we would be much better equipped to identify problems as they arise. So, let's do that.

Take a moment to think about your dog's normal day and make note of the following. These notes are great to reflect back on every few months (or sooner if you think you notice changes) and see if there may be some changes you didn't recognize because they happened gradually. It is also beneficial to update your records as needed to ensure you always have an accurate "snapshot" of how your dog is functioning.

Today's Date: _____

How much are they eating and drinking?

_____

_____

_____

_____

How much exercise does your dog get on a typical day? Make note of their energy level and how far/long they can walk.

_____

_____

_____

_____

Does your dog like to be groomed? Are there any spots they don't like touched?

_____

_____

_____

_____

Next, have someone else walk your dog for you while you watch them move.

Do you notice them favouring a limb or limping (lameness)? Is their head bobbing up and down?

A head bob can be an indication that they are trying to keep weight off of one of their front limbs. To determine which front leg they are trying to protect - look at which front leg is touching the ground when the head moves up. The head will rise when they are trying not to put their weight through the leg that is touching the ground.

_____

_____

_____

_____

Do they look like they are hiking up one of their back hips as they walk? That would be an indication that they are trying to keep weight off of one of their back legs. Again, the side that is being lifted is the side that the dog is trying to avoid putting weight on.

_____

_____

_____

_____

Continue to watch the way your dog moves. Can they sit squarely? Meaning can they sit with both legs tucked in evenly? An inability to do this could be an indication of weakness in the back end or pain in the back legs.

Thabiso on the left sitting sloppy vs. Beau on the right sitting square.

_____

_____

_____

_____

How quickly can they go from lying down to sitting to standing? Do they hesitate?

Hesitation can be a sign of pain or weakness.

_____

_____

_____

_____

Lastly, take some time to purposefully touch your dog. Run your hands over the limbs and down their back. Make note of any warm or cold spots, any changes in the coat or any lumps or bumps that you may feel. This will give you a starting point if you find something new later on. Also note any areas that seem sore to your touch or seem "tight", which may indicate a muscle "knot" or muscle spasm.

_____

_____

_____

_____

~ 4 ~

Pain

Signs of Pain

Many well-intentioned dog owners miss signs of pain in their dogs. Vocalization (i.e., whimpering or crying) of pain is often a good indicator that pain is at a very high level. However, many dogs that are below a certain threshold may never vocalize pain. That's because dogs do not process pain like humans do. If you've ever sought out medical care for an injury you've likely been asked to rate your pain on a scale of 0 to 10. Dogs do not operate on this scale. They go from 0-6 "I'm feeling fine! Oh look! Squirrel" to 7-10 "oh my gosh the house is on fire!" type of pain. It is hypothesized that this is evolutionary as dogs are pack animals and they do not want to be perceived as weak and dropped from the pack. So, they carry on and work through that pain. There is little middle ground when it comes to pain in dogs. However, if we are watching for the signs, we can more readily identify those lower levels of pain and do something to help before the pain becomes worse or becomes chronic.

A common sign of pain is lameness, but many owners will often misinterpret this as being something other than pain. However, if you stop to ask yourself why your dog is not using a leg properly why would that be? If a dog is unwilling to use their leg normally or put their weight through that leg, likely it hurts to do so, but because the dog is not crying or whimpering it can easily be midjudged.

This can become a cycle - a dog may have a period of lameness but then they recover and walk normally. We assume the pain and the problem is gone. Then they start to limp again and this time the lameness might last a little longer but once again they recover. If we never do anything to figure out what the source of the lameness is, we may be allowing a chronic condition to develop. This is very common in the early stages of arthritis.

Also common in the early stages of arthritis is a dog who is stiff and lame when first getting up and moving around but then warms out of it and starts to move normally. That initial lameness that does not last is likely pain

Other signs of pain may include a change in behaviour, such as the dog no longer coming to greet you at the front door when you get home from work. It could be the dog no longer jumps up on the furniture or on the bed the way they used to. Maybe the dog always went downstairs or upstairs during the day and now they're staying on the same level of the house. Possibly these activities that they once did regularly have now become painful and in order to limit their pain they're avoiding doing them. They might also seem very irritable around other animals and pets in the home and may display this by exhibiting aggressive behaviour (e.g., snapping, growling).

Henry likes be close to his mom. A change in this could tell you he is hurting.

A dog that was once very independent but now wishes to cuddle more could be in pain. Or the dog that was very snuggly may be avoiding you or your touch. Maybe your dog has lost interest in the activities that used to be fun for them, like going for walks or playing with toys

A dog that has a sudden change in appetite may also be in pain. Often dogs who are in pain will eat less. If their eating habits change, it could be due to pain in their mouth making it difficult to chew, or pain elsewhere in their body disrupting their appetite. There is a huge benefit to ensuring your senior dog has regular dental check-ups. This can help identify things like gingivitis (gum disease), tooth loss/decay or infection. It's estimated that 2/3s of dogs over the age of 3 have some sort of dental disease.[1] So, if your dog is a senior, chances are they have some sort of changes happening with their teeth.

A change in sleeping pattern is another sign of pain. A dog either may sleep more in order to rest the area or they might be restless and have more difficulty getting comfortable and going to sleep.

A very observant owner may notice their dog starting to breathe more quickly but with shallow breaths. A change in breathing may become more noticeable if the dog starts to pant without doing any activity.

Sam at 17. Panting or other breathing problems without a known cause, could be a sign of pain.

If you are concerned that your dog might be in pain, it is advisable to seek out an assessment from your dog care professional to determine the source of the pain and how to treat it.

Pain Management

Beyond medications, there are many different modalities that can help your dog with their pain. Sometimes these are offered by your primary veterinarian. Often times, however, you will need to seek out other pet care professionals such as chiropractors, canine rehab therapists or canine physical therapists, and other alternative practitioners. When seeking out care from non-veterinarians, it is good practice to review the education of the individual you are considering working with to make sure they have the knowledge to use any of these modalities safely.

Acupuncture. Acupuncture can be helpful for relieving soft tissue pain and also internal pain. Acupuncture is a type of Traditional Chinese Medicine that aims to restore the body's natural energy flow called qi (pronounced *chi*). Very fine needles are used to stimulate specific acupuncture points and are thought to restore energy flow.

Tanner getting acupuncture.

Research now suggests that acupuncture works by causing the brain to release endogenous opioids (i.e., serotonin and norepinephrine) which help to reduce pain in the body. There is also likely some amount of placebo effect from acupuncture. And yes, the placebo effect can impact dogs and their owners! More about that at the end of this chapter.

Laser. Laser stands for Light Amplification by Stimulated Emission of Radiation. Laser uses light energy to affect the tissues it is aimed at. Laser helps pain by releasing endorphins. It also helps indirectly by stimulating cartilage production and the creation of new blood vessels, improving immune function, healing wounds, accelerating the inflammatory phase of healing and reducing oxidative stress.

Laser can help with many conditions that cause pain. Some examples are arthritis, nerve pain, tendon or ligament injuries, wounds, muscle spasms and skin wounds.

Gizmo having laser treatment.

Massage. Most of us know the relaxing effects of massage first hand. Our dogs are no different. Massage can help with relaxation. This is great for senior dogs who may have developed anxiety. A relaxation massage can help decrease a dog's blood pressure and heart rate. Massage is also beneficial for pain relief. Massage can increase blood flow to a muscle, reduce muscle tone, and separate the fibres of muscles all helping to reduce muscular pain.

TENS. TENS stands for Transcutaneous Electrical Neuromuscular Stimulation. An electrical current is applied to the body for the sole purpose of pain relief. TENS helps to decrease pain by blocking other sensory signals to the brain (i.e., the brain feels the electrical stimulation instead of the pain), stimulating the release of endorphins and opiates and reducing other chemicals in the body that contribute to pain.

Ultrasound. Ultrasound transmits energy to tissues through a sound wave. When ultrasound is used at settings that increase tissue temperature it can increase metabolic rate, reduce pain and muscle spasms, reduce the rate at which nerves transmit pain, increase circulation and increase soft tissue flexibility. When used at settings that don't cause a rise in temperature, ultrasound can then be used over areas where increasing temperature would have a negative effect, such as over plastic or metal implants, areas with reduced sensation (i.e., could not tell if the ultrasound was too hot) or over inflamed tissues. These non-thermal settings have effects on the different stages of tissue healing, thus decreasing pain.

Ultrasound can help reduce pain when used on the following conditions: muscle spasm, trigger points, tendon, muscle or ligament injuries, fractures, osteoarthritis and wounds

Manual therapy. Manual therapy is a broad term that encompasses many techniques that help to improve joint range of motion and flexibility, promote relaxation, and reduce swelling and pain. Manual therapy techniques include both mobilizations and manipulations, which are often used by chiropractors and physiotherapists as part of a treatment program. Mobilization of a joint is done manually (without a machine) by oscillating the joint. A manipulation is a high velocity thrust (i.e., fast and quick) movement of the joint. Manipulations are what are typically thought of when discussing chiropractic treatment.

Pulsed Electromagnetic Field Therapy (PEMF). Magnetic field therapy is thought to work by changing the charge (positive or negative) on damaged cells. When cells are damaged, they do not use oxygen properly. When the cell charge is changed by a magnetic field, oxygen use is improved. PEMF enhances cartilage repair and increases the production of collagen and bone. It can be used to treat fractures, inflammation, muscle spasms, tendon injuries and wounds, as well as post-operatively. By promoting healing, PEMF has an indirect effect on decreasing pain.

PEMF therapies can come in the form of beds, coats or loops and/or pads placed on the dog.

Dexter lying on a PEMF bed.

Electrical Muscle Stimulation (EMS). EMS uses an electrical current to stimulate a muscle to contract. This can be highly beneficial following a surgery as pain will often prevent a muscle from working properly. When a muscle contacts, blood flow increases which reduces swelling and causes an endorphin release, which helps reduce pain.

EMS can also be used on the following conditions to help decrease pain: joint swelling, tendon injury, fractures, muscle spasms and skin ulcers.

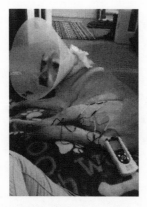

Maggie with the muscle stim on after knee surgery

Radial Shockwave. Radial shockwave targets tissues with a pressure wave using pneumatic technology in the shockwave head. This pressure wave is absorbed and spread through the body. Radial shockwave does not affect pain directly, but rather has an effect on healing and inflammation which results in decreased pain. Some of the healing effects include improved blood flow and growth factor release, increasing the number of stem cells that effect bone growth and blocking some of the parts of the inflammatory process.

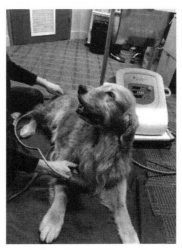

Puzzle enjoying shockwave

Radial shockwave should not be confused with focused shockwave which is more powerful, reaches deeper tissues (i.e., organs), carries a higher risk of negative effects and can be painful.

Hot and cold therapy. Most of us are familiar with using heating pads and ice packs on achy muscles and injuries.

Heat can be effective in reducing pain by increasing blood flow, reducing muscle spasms, increasing tissue flexibility, and relaxing muscles. Heat is something most owners can easily use on their dogs at home. It is best applied when there is no acute inflammation (i.e., not used during the first few days after an injury or surgery). A good rule of thumb to follow is if the area is already hot or warm to the touch, we don't want to make it hotter, so heat should not be used.

Owners should be wary about applying heat to a dog that may have reduced sensation. This can lead to a burn because the dog won't try to get away from the heat if it is too hot. Heat should be applied for no longer than 15-20 minutes and then removed.

Cold therapy is also well within an owner's ability to use. It can help to reduce pain by decreasing inflammation and swelling and by slowing nerve conduction (i.e., the pain signals to the brain). Opposite to applying heat, it is best applied in the first 48 hours after an acute injury or surgery or anytime there is heat and swelling. Ice is typically applied for 10-20 minutes. Applying ice for too long can actually lead to an increase in blood flow to the area which is opposite to the effects desired. Again, take precautions when using cold in areas with reduced feeling to avoid causing injury. It is also good practice to provide a barrier like a towel between the ice/cold pack and your dog's body.

When using hot or cold therapy with your dog, if you are unsure you are making the right decision about its use, check in with your veterinarian or other dog care professional to determine if it is appropriate.

The Placebo Effect

The placebo effect in dogs works differently than in humans, but in both cases relies on the human to report a change in symptoms. Dogs cannot tell us when they are feeling unwell or when they are hurting. We have to rely on their behaviour to speak for them. Studies show that both vets and owners are not good at determining if medications, especially for arthritis, have made a positive impact.[2,3] It is rare that more objective measures are used to determine if a medication has worked. An example of an objective measure is a stance analyser that uses a computer system to determine how much a dog is using each leg. Our biases are removed because the computer does the assessment for us.

The placebo effect occurs in dogs because we are invested in seeing our pets improve. It does us no good to think what we've tried to do to help our dog doesn't work but we can use this to our advantage. Believing our dog feels better might give us the confidence to do more with our dog. This may lead to more stimulation and more activity for our dog and may also keep us from doing too much for our dog such as lifting them up the 2 steps into the house when they can do it themselves.

The placebo effect can benefit us unknowingly in other ways by changing our behaviour if we are working with a vet or canine rehab therapist. If the goal is to reduce arthritis pain, we may also start doing other things that will help our dog. For example, we might be more mindful of what we are feeding our dog leading to weight loss, which can also help arthritis pain.

However, we also need to be careful that the placebo effect does not cause harm to our dog. If we think they are doing better and then suddenly increase their activity too much, we can actually make them worse.

It is important to be aware of the placebo effect with our older dogs so that we can attempt to be a bit more skeptical of what might be making our dogs better in order to avoid making them worse.

~ 5 ~

Arthritis

Arthritis affects 1 out of 4 adult dogs, and up to 4 out of 5 senior dogs.[4] It can be very easy to blame many of the changes that happen to senior dogs on arthritis, but without doing anything further, the dog will usually continue to get worse. In order to help our senior dogs that do have arthritis, it is important to know what arthritis actually is.

What is arthritis?

Arthritis is the term most people use when referring to osteoarthritis. *Osteo* refers to bones and *arth* to joints. The -itis on the end refers to inflammation. Normal, healthy joints have a smooth layer of cartilage at the ends of the bones. When that cartilage layer starts to wear without being replaced and repaired properly, that's when a problem starts. The new cartilage is not as thick or smooth, has gaps and does not glide as nicely. The joint space, or the space between the bone ends that make up a joint, gets smaller and there is more rubbing between the bones. The bone underneath the cartilage is exposed, and the body responds by trying to build new bone but this new bone is not smooth.

This leads to a cycle of pain and inflammation in the joint. An owner will often then limit how much activity the dog does for fear of hurting the dog which leads to weakness. This weakness further increases pain and inflammation because the joint isn't moving as much and there is more shear (i.e., rubbing of the bone ends in the joint) due to less muscle support, thus leading to more inactivity and so on. If nothing is done, a downward cycle begins.

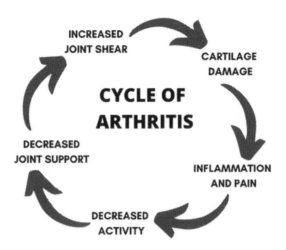

In the past, it was thought that osteoarthritis was strictly a wear-and-tear condition in which the joint wears down over time with use. We now know that osteoarthritis is not always caused by wear. It can also be caused by a previous injury such as a ligament tear or surgery. This is one of the reasons why a young dog can also have arthritis.

Degenerative joint disease is another, yet potentially scary, name for arthritis. *Degenerate* means to diminish in quality.[5] How horrible is that?! However, arthritis is often a common part of aging, much like greying of the hair or wrinkling of the skin. It is not an illness.

Risk factors for developing arthritis are varied. The biggest risk factor is age and the older a dog is the more likely they are to have or develop arthritis. Of course, age is out of anyone's control. Other risks include obesity, sex (males more likely to develop arthritis than females), previous injuries (i.e., hip dysplasia, cranial cruciate ligament tear) and breed. Weight control and preventing injuries are well within reason for an owner to control.

It is also important to know that osteoarthritis cannot be cured. It can be managed by reducing risk factors, modifying activity and diet and treating symptoms. Early identification is important in order to treat arthritis appropriately and limit its progression.

There is some evidence[6] that suggests by reversing the early joint changes that typically lead to osteoarthritis such as joint inflammation, we might actually be able to prevent it from occurring. Strategies to achieve this include[7] managing inflammation (such as with anti-inflammatories), stimulating joint healing, strengthening the muscles around (and therefore the support) of a joint, maintaining the full range of motion of a joint and joint supplementation. We will discuss all of these.

Arthritis on an X-ray

Was arthritis unexpectedly found on an x-ray for your dog? Does the amount of arthritis your vet saw on the x-ray match how well your dog is doing? Many things that are found on x-rays are not actually problematic. When treating arthritis, it is important to treat the dog and not the x-ray.

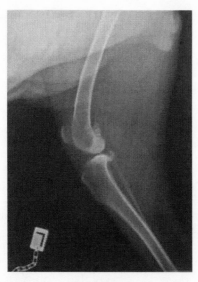

Knee joint x-ray

What this means is if your dog is moving well and has no signs of pain, your dog likely does not need much treatment. This is important to keep in mind, as the amount of arthritis in the joint will not change once treatment starts. What can be changed and improved is your dog's level of pain, strength, flexibility and balance, as well as how they are functioning day to day.

Keep in mind, the severity of the arthritis on an x-ray is not directly related to how your dog is doing. It is possible to have minimal amounts of arthritis on an x-ray while your dog is in a significant amount of pain. Similarly, your dog may have significant arthritis on an x-ray, while experiencing minimal pain. There is not a good correlation between x-ray findings and pain or function.

Treatments for Arthritis

Medication

The most common type of medication used to control pain in canine osteoarthritis are NSAIDS or nonsteroidal anti-inflammatories.[8] These medications are designed to reduce the inflammation in a joint and thus the pain the dog feels. Commonly prescribed NSAIDs in veterinary medicine include carprofen (Novox or Rimadyl), deracoxib (Deramaxx), firocoxib (Previcox) and meloxicam (Metacam). These medications should not be given to a dog unless prescribed by a veterinarian after a proper examination to ensure this type of medication is appropriate for your dog. Serious side effects can include issues with the stomach, liver and kidneys. Watch for diarrhea, loss of appetite, vomiting, lethargy or any other changes and follow-up with your vet as needed. Often these side effects are seen within the first few weeks of starting an NSAID. The frequency of negative side effects is somewhat unclear for NSAIDs in dogs, but research suggests the risks are low, even with long term use, especially when compared to humans.[9,10] It has been suggested[11] that bloodwork be repeated every 3 months for dogs over 10 and every 6-12 months for younger dogs. Discuss with your vet how your dog should be monitored if using NSAIDs.

Owners should not use NSAIDs designed for human use with their dogs as this could be fatal. Pain signs in your dog should be noted before starting this type of medication and then reassessed 2-3 weeks later to determine if the medication is effective. If this type of medication is going to be used long-term, it is also best to monitor chronic pain symptoms to see if the daily dosage can be reduced.

Other medications a veterinarian may prescribe for arthritis pain are primarily aimed towards decreasing chronic pain. They are also often used with NSAIDs. Opioids may be prescribed such as Morphine and Codeine. Pregabalin and Gabapentin are both anticonvulsant medications that can treat chronic pain and nerve pain. These medications can have significant side effects and, again, should be discussed with your veterinarian.

Injections

There are injectable disease modifying osteoarthritic agents that can help. A disease modifying agent changes how a disease affects the body, rather than directly treating the symptoms. In the case of arthritis, this means the drug has an effect on the joint itself.

Adequan is an injection into the muscle or under the skin that helps protect the cartilage and reduce inflammation. It does not repair cartilage that has already changed due to arthritis. Because Adequan does not repair cartilage, it is best suited for dogs in the early stages of arthritis.

Cartrophen is another injection that goes under the skin. It works by stopping the breakdown of cartilage, encouraging new cartilage growth, increasing joint lubrication and stimulating the production of antioxidants.

Hyaluronic acid is normally found in joints and lubricates the joint, like oil does in a car. In joints with arthritis the hyaluronic acid molecule is smaller than normal leading to poor lubrication of the joint. An injection of hyaluronic acid is thought to increase lubrication and cushioning in the joint, thus reducing pain, decreasing inflammation and slowing down the progression of arthritis.

Platelet Rich Plasma (PRP) treatment involves separating plasma from a dog's own blood and then injecting it into the arthritic joint. Platelets contain growth factors that aid in healing which can be beneficial for healing cartilage, bone, tendons and ligaments. It is thought that PRP reduces arthritis pain by reducing inflammation.

Joint Supplements

Covered in more detail in chapter 9, joint supplements help to feed the cartilage and support the health of the joint. Buyer beware though as supplements do not need to be proven to work in order to be sold to the public. Ingredients that owners should seek out are glucosamine, polyunsaturated fatty acids/fish oil, chondroitin sulfate or green lipped mussels, as there is research to support their effectiveness. When in doubt, discuss any product you are thinking of giving to your dog with your veterinarian. When starting your dog on a joint supplement, keep in mind that it can take up to 2-4 months of giving your dog a joint supplement to see a change in your dog.

Physical Activity

An arthritic dog needs to keep moving but determining how much exercise is appropriate can be challenging. Rule of thumb is no bout of exercise should make the dog worse. So, if you take your dog out for a walk, they should be no more lame returning home than they were going out.

Phoebe out for a walk.

You should avoid sudden increases in the amount or intensity of exercise or you risk causing sudden episodes of lameness and pain in your dog. This includes playing rough with other dogs or chasing balls. Different terrain may also unwittingly increase the challenge as well. A 30-minute walk on the sidewalk in your neighbourhood is not as difficult as a 30-minute hike on hilly, uneven terrain.

Often owners will think that because their dog will still do these activities, that they are safe for their dog to do. This really is not the case. Many dogs do not know when they have had enough or should limit themselves. If you've ever been in charge of a small child you know this principle already! We don't let young kids go wildly jumping off of furniture or wrestle aggressively because they can (and usually do) get hurt. We should treat our dogs, especially senior dogs, the same way.

For your daily walks you may want to consider breaking up a walk that was once 30-minutes long into two shorter walks of 15-minutes each, or build a rest break into your walk before you turn around to head home.

"Motion is lotion" is a commonly used phrase when discussing activity and arthritis. The fluid in our joints, called synovial fluid, acts like a lubricant. If the joints are still and not moving, that fluid does not get coated over the bones of the joint to do its job. Dogs should be encouraged to move even when they might have very painful arthritis. Failing to do so may be causing our dog more harm than good in the long run.

And lastly, consider the importance of muscular support to joints. Joints themselves without ligament, tendon and muscles are not stable and will move in every direction. (I like to think of the skeletons we hang up at Halloween as an example of a skeleton without support). It is the muscles that stabilize the joint so that there is less shear between the bone ends. By keeping the muscles strong we can then limit excessive movement of the joint which can increase pain and worsen arthritis.

If your dog was a sporting dog in their younger days, they may still be able to keep up some of their old past times. Ideal sports for older dogs may include scent detection, barn hunt, rally obedience or a trick class! Some of the faster paced activities may need to be retired such as agility, flyball, dock diving and luring. Try to be creative and incorporate some of the elements of your dog's favourite activities into your routine, such as swimming if they like to do dock diving or some low jumps if they were into agility.

For more examples of exercises that you can do with your senior dog, see chapter 10.

~ 6 ~

Common Old Dog Issues

Weakness

Weakness is a typical trait of senior dogs. Unfortunately, because weakness is so common in older dogs it is often considered normal and not addressed. It is important to determine the reason why your dog might be becoming weak as there is the possibility that there may be an underlying disease or illness you are not aware of. Have your dog assessed by your veterinarian to rule out any potential cause of weakness that should be treated medically (such as a heart condition, infection or hormone imbalances).

OLD ≠ WEAK

In both humans and in dogs, there is a loss of muscle mass and function with age. There is no universally accepted reason for why this occurs but research suggests that the body does not repair muscle as well with age and, generally, activity levels decrease with age even without any underlying illness or disease.

What is important for our dogs as they get older, much like humans, is to continue to be active and to eat quality foods. In the absence of any other disease, it has been suggested that adequate levels of dietary protein can help prevent muscle loss.[12]

Cancer

Just like humans, dogs can be diagnosed with cancer. And like humans, the likelihood of being diagnosed with cancer increases with age with up to 50% of older dogs being diagnosed.[13,14] Cancer is the leading cause of death in dogs over the age of 10 and 1 in 4 dogs will die from cancer.[8,9] Dogs are susceptible to many of the same types of cancer that humans are. There are certainly breeds that are more disposed to certain types of cancers than others but reviewing each breed is beyond the scope of this book. If an owner is wishing to learn more about their dog's breed specific risk, it is suggested that they research their specific breed. Keep in mind that a higher risk of getting cancer does not mean your dog will develop cancer, nor does a lower risk protect them from developing it.

The Animal Cancer Foundation[15] cites the following as warning signs for dog owners. If you notice any of these signs in your dog, you should see your vet.

- *Oral odour* may be due to oral cancer. Difficulty chewing or a change in food preferences (i.e., hard vs. soft) would be another sign.

- *Straining to urinate* or blood in the urine often indicates a bladder infection. If symptoms do not resolve with treatment, your vet should investigate further to determine the source of the problem.

- *Lameness* without obvious cause (such as caused by running or playing) especially if it does not resolve with rest.

- *Coughing* can be caused by many things, but should always be investigated by a vet.

- *Unexplained bleeding* coming from the nose, gums or mouth. Blood in stool or urine should also be brought to a vet's attention.

- *Chronic Vomiting or diarrhea* without a known cause.

- *Chronic weight loss* when you are not trying to help your dog lose weight.

- *Abdominal distension* in which the belly or abdomen becomes enlarged quickly.

- *An enlarged or changing lump.* Often found while petting or grooming. A vet can take a sample to determine if the lump is cancerous.

- *Swollen lymph nodes.* Lymph nodes are found throughout the body, but are most easily felt under the jaw bone or behind the knee.

Many of the above signs can have many different causes that are not cancer related but should be brought to the attention of your veterinarian for appropriate evaluation. Often problems that are found early are easier to treat - both for your dog and your wallet.

Dogs are susceptible to many different types of cancers. Again, it is beyond the purview of this book to review them all. Osteosarcoma and soft tissue sarcoma will be covered in this book as they can easily mimic other muscle/bone/joint issues. Sarcomas account for approximately 10-15% of malignant tumours in dogs, 20% occurring in bone and 80% in soft tissue (i.e., muscles, tendons, fat, nerves).

Osteosarcoma is the most common canine bone tumour and usually occurs in the humerus (upper front leg) close to the shoulder, in the radius (forearm bone) close to the dog's wrist or in the hind end either in the femur (thigh bone) close to the knee or tibia (shin bone). Often osteosarcoma is said to be "away from elbow, close to the knee". The front limbs of dogs are affected twice as often as the hind limbs.[16]

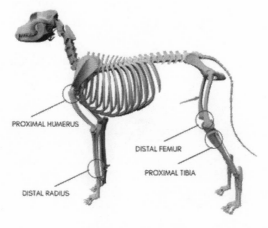

Common sites of osteosarcomas

Despite osteosarcoma being the most common canine bone tumour, it is still relatively rare with estimated incidence anywhere between 0.2% and 10.7% depending on breed.[17,18]

The earliest signs of osteosarcoma are usually progressive swelling and mild, intermittent lameness,[19] then progressing to more consistent and severe lameness. This highlights the importance of re-examination by a veterinarian if treatment for a suspected orthopaedic injury does not improve as expected.

The survival rate for osteosarcoma in dogs is very poor, 1-year survival rate is approximately 45%[20] and more than half of those surviving after a year will develop cancer metastasis (i.e., cancer that moves to other areas of the body).[21] Dogs who have metastases at the time of diagnosis have poorer outcomes.

Treatment options that may be presented by a veterinarian are limb amputation, surgery to remove the tumour (likely accompanied by other procedures to stabilize the bone), chemotherapy, radiation, immunotherapy and palliative treatment.

Soft tissue sarcoma (STS) is a broad term which encompasses many types of cancers such as hemangiosarcomas, fibrosarcomas, peripheral nerve sheath tumours and histiocytic sarcomas. Symptoms are often vague for many of these cancers, so if your dog is having abnormal, unexplained symptoms, a trip to the vet is warranted. STS can often invade the tissues surrounding them but do not usually spread to other areas of the body. Treatment is usually surgery to remove the tumour and possibly radiation or chemotherapy.

Incontinence

Leaking bladders and urinating or pooping in the house when your dog is house trained is considered incontinence. Incontinence is the lack of voluntary control of the bowel and bladder. But why does it happen? There are multiple reasons.

In senior dogs, weakness is a big cause. The bladder is a large muscle that holds urine. When the muscle is contracting it holds urine. When it relaxes, it allows urination. If the muscle is weak the bladder can leak. Often this leaking occurs when there is extra stress on the bladder, such as a very full bladder or from an external force, like barking or jumping. Another way that muscle weakness causes incontinence is if the dog is too weak to get up to let the owner know that they need to go out to go to the bathroom. And if the dog can't make it outside to do their business, they end up doing it inside.

The bladder is also supported inside the body by other muscles. If that support network of muscles becomes too short/tight in some places or too weak in others, it can prevent the bladder from working as well as it should. A good analogy for this is a garden hose on the ground flowing with water. If you step on the hose, the flow of water stops. But if that same hose was on soft, boggy ground and we stepped on the hose, there would still be water flowing out of the end. The same goes for the flow of urine out of the bladder and the muscles that support it. If the muscles that support the bladder are weak, urine can still leak out.

In addition to the muscles inside the abdomen, the external core muscles also play an important role in supporting the bladder and internal muscles. Often dogs who have been spayed or have been pregnant have weak abdominals. Other causes of abdominal muscle weakness include abdominal surgeries, bowel surgeries and early spay. In fact, 90% of incontinent bitches are spayed[22] and 20% of spayed bitches have urinary incontinence.[23] Rarely do male dogs have incontinence whether neutered or not. It is not entirely known why spayed females more often experience incontinence, but theories include a decrease in muscle contractility[24] and a decrease in estrogen.

Another common cause of incontinence in senior dogs are back and nerve problems. If the nerve signals going to the bladder are interrupted it can cause the bladder muscle to not work as effectively, as the nerve is what tells the muscle what to do. If the nerves going from the bladder to the brain are not functioning properly, the dog may not actually realize when they need to go to the bathroom.

So, what causes the nerves to not work properly? Simply think of the nerves as the telephone wire connection that allows the brain to talk to the muscles. If the message is cut off or the message becomes too quiet, the bladder and the brain have difficulty talking to each other. This can happen as changes occur in the back and, more specifically, the joints in the back. Nerves branch off of the spinal cord and travel to the muscles they control. To get to the muscles, the nerves pass through canals between the bones in the spine. If those canals are narrowed from changes due to aging like arthritis, some pressure can be applied to the nerves, preventing a clear message from being sent through the nerve.

There are things that you can do to help decrease or stop incontinence. If your dog is overweight that can increase the likelihood of incontinence as there is more pressure on the bladder muscles and the muscles that support the bladder. Decreasing body weight (discussed in the next chapter) can help decrease the pressure on the muscles.

If your dog is constipated this can also be problematic. If your dog has too much stool in their body it can actually change the position of the bladder, which can affect how it functions. If your dog is straining to try to poop it increases the pressure inside of their abdomen and this can lead to a leaky bladder. Ways to address this would be to try to increase fibre in the diet (such as adding canned pumpkin or green beans to the diet) and adding a bit of water to the food (especially if your dog is on a kibble diet).

Try to limit other things that can increase the pressure on the bladder. This includes increasing the opportunities that your dog has to go to the bathroom so that the bladder isn't too full. If your dog is a barker, try to limit the triggers for barking (e.g., posting a sign asking that the doorbell not be rung). If your dog is a jumper, try to limit the opportunities to jump. If your dog tends to be incontinent overnight, think about limiting their opportunity to have water in the few hours before bed.

Also consider having your dog assessed by a canine rehab therapist. They can look for muscles that might be tight or weak and help to address these. Incontinence can also be treated with the help of your veterinarian and medications.

Vertigo

In dogs, vertigo is called *idiopathic geriatric vestibulitis*. Idiopathic means that there is no apparent cause. Geriatric, of course, means senior. The vestibular system maintains posture and balance of the head and body (i.e., knowing which way is straight and/or forward). Vestibulitis means that there are errors happening in this system and the brain has difficulty orienting itself to the horizon (i.e., it doesn't know where straight is).

The symptoms of vertigo come on quickly. What you would see in your dog if they were experiencing vestibulitis are a head tilt, unsteady walking or falling over, circling in one direction, vomiting, and rapidly bouncing or jerking eyes (nystagmus). Your dog may also refuse to get up, as moving around may exacerbate their symptoms.

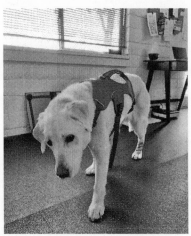

Hailey has some classic signs of geriatric vestibular disease: head down and slightly tilted. She is also unsteady on her feet.

Often no medical treatment is required, though if your dog is not eating or drinking that is cause for concern and a visit to your veterinarian is warranted. They may also benefit from medications to help ease nausea or help them relax.

A canine rehab therapist can also help to reduce symptoms by performing a technique called the Epley maneuver, which is used in humans to treat vertigo. The theory behind the Epley maneuver is that vertigo is caused by crystals that have moved into the wrong part of the inner ear and are sending incorrect messages to the brain. The Epley maneuver attempts to remove these crystals from the inner ear. This technique involves moving a dog's body and head through a sequence of positions designed to clear the canal of the inner ear. If after the Epley maneuver has been performed your dog still has balance issues, a canine rehab therapist can also help by designing an exercise program that helps your dog regain their balance.

Intervertebral Disc Disease (IVDD)

Changes to the vertebral discs between the bones/vertebrae of the spine are normal with aging. The vertebral discs act as cushions in the spine. They are moveable and soft. They have a jelly-like filling (nucleus pulposus) and a tough but flexible outer layer (annulus fibrosus). With age, the outer layer gets thicker and less flexible. The jelly starts to dry up and become more like dried toothpaste. The outer, thickened layers begin to push against the spinal cord causing Hansen Type 2 intervertebral disc disease. Hansen Type 1 IVDD will not be discussed in this book as it usually affects younger dogs.

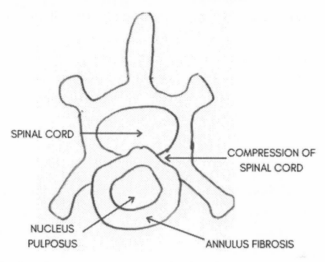

IVDD Type 2 results in compression of the spinal cord, resulting in progressive functional decline.

Hansen IVDD Type 2 causes progressive decline over weeks, months or even years. Symptoms depend on where the spinal cord is being compressed. As discussed in the section on incontinence, the nerves bring messages from the spinal cord to the muscles. If the message isn't getting through properly, the muscles don't work as they should. The dog may be wobbly, drag their feet or even knuckle over on their paws so that they actually walk on the top sides of their feet, be incontinent or develop some degree of paralysis. If the compressed area is in the neck, the dog may be reluctant to lift their head as this would further compress the spinal cord. If the compression is further down the back, the dog may have a hunched back. Other common signs are a reluctance to exercise, rise, do stairs or they may appear stiff. There is typically some degree of pain with IVDD.

Treatment for IVDD includes lifestyle changes such as weight reduction and activity modification and medications to reduce inflammation. A canine rehab therapist can also help with modalities such as acupuncture, manual therapy and exercise. Surgery is not indicated for Type 2 IVDD.

Spondylosis

Spondylosis (or spondylosis deformans) is a degenerative condition of the spine that often occurs as a result of intervertebral disk disease (IVDD). Unlike osteoarthritis, it is not an inflammatory condition. It is thought that the body makes extra bone (bone spurs) on the ends of the vertebral bones as a sort of bridge to make the spine more stable. This instability is thought to be caused by vertebral bone deformities, trauma or discospondylitis (an infection of the disc).[25] However, because the bone is stable and unmoveable, it makes the spine stiff in the areas where this happens.

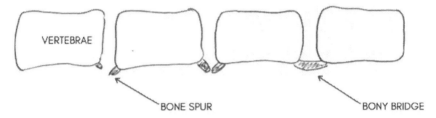

Spondylosis results in bony bridging between vertebrae, leading to a stiff joint in the spine.

Usually, spondylosis is found by accident on an x-ray. It is more common in older dogs, and affects more areas of the spine with age. Often there may be no signs and symptoms that your dog has developed spondylosis. When there are signs and symptoms you may notice stiffness in the back as mentioned above, lameness, changes in how your dog walks or pain. The cause of symptoms, when they do occur, would be a bone spur growing closely to a nerve exiting the spinal cord causing compression on the nerve.

Treatment depends on if a dog has any signs or symptoms. If your dog is in pain, discuss whether pain medications are warranted with your vet. Weight loss if your dog is overweight to decrease the stress on your dog's back is important. Canine rehab is also beneficial for improving flexibility, increasing the strength of the abdominal and back muscles to support the spine as well as pain relieving modalities like laser, PEMF and acupuncture.

~ 7 ~

Behaviour changes

Canine Cognitive Dysfunction

Canine cognitive dysfunction (CCD), or canine cognitive dysfunction syndrome (CDS), is commonly referred to as canine dementia. CCD is similar to human Alzheimer's disease. It is classified as a *neurodegenerative disease* because there are changes to the cells (neurons) in the brain. CCD affects up to 60% of dogs and usually the dog is over the age of 11 years.[26] No breed seems to be more at risk, but small dogs are often more affected than large dogs because they usually have a longer life span.[27]

CCD is diagnosed by ruling out other ailments (e.g., brain tumours, hormone imbalances, etc.). The diagnosis is then made on the basis of observed symptoms by the owner and their vet by following the DISHAA acronym[28]:

D - **D**isorientation - staring off, circling, getting lost in familiar places, waiting at the hinge side of a door, falling off things

I - altered social **I**nteractions - more attention seeking or withdrawn, being frightened of familiar people or animals, aggression

S - altered **S**leep–wake cycles - mixing up days and nights, night pacing

H - **H**ouse soiling and loss of other learned behaviours - not recognizing name, forgetting routines,

A - altered **A**ctivity levels - more sedentary, barking when they wouldn't normally or not barking when they normally would, repetitive behaviours

A - increasing **A**nxiety - fear, anxiety, depression

There is no cure for CCD. There are medications that are designed to slow the progression of the disease or manage symptoms. Research also suggests that diets rich in antioxidants can also be beneficial.[29,30,31] Without getting too technical, antioxidants can be thought of as cleaners that help remove free-radicals from the body so they can't damage cells. Free radicals occur in our body naturally as a biproduct of our cells doing what they should be doing. Free radicals can also occur as a result of stress, poor diet and pollution. They cause damage to cells, resulting in inflammation and increasing the risk of certain diseases such as CCD.

Antioxidants owners may look for that are beneficial for dogs with CCD are vitamin E, vitamin C, carnitine and alpha-lipoic acid (ALA). Sources of these antioxidants are:

- Vitamin E – nuts and seeds

- Vitamin C – citrus fruits, strawberries, green peppers, broccoli and green leafy vegetables

- Carnitine – beef, chicken and in supplement form

- ALA – spinach, beef hearts, broccoli and in supplement form

It is best to work with a veterinarian or someone who is knowledgeable about pet food science to ensure you are providing your dog with healthy amounts of antioxidants. This is especially true for supplement forms of antioxidants. Too much can be harmful in some cases.

There are many strategies an owner of a dog with CCD may use to help care for them. There is no one recommendation that will work for every dog.

For dogs that become disoriented, providing easy access to their bedding, food and water is helpful. You likely thought about puppy proofing your home when you brought them home for the first time. It's time to do the same thing for your senior. Try to limit areas they can get into but not back out of (e.g., a space between a wall and a couch). Many dogs with CCD will forget how to back up. Placing food and water bowls in corners may help prevent them from walking over them. Raise the bowls up to an optimal height to encourage them to continue to eat and drink.

Be aware of doors that open inwards. It is very common for dogs with CCD to stand at the hinges waiting for the door to be opened. Be patient and see if you can lure them to the correct spot with treats.

Gerard looking to the oven to be let outside.

Continue to get your dog into the sunshine during the day if they are starting to confuse days and nights. The exposure to sunlight can help regulate the sleep-wake cycle. This does not mean you have to be going for a walk if your dog is struggling to get around. Sitting outside with them on a nice day, or a ride in a wagon can be beneficial.

Because your dog may no longer recognize when they need to go to the bathroom you may be dealing with more accidents. Diapers and belly bands are one way to minimize mess. A belly band is an option for male dogs and warps around the waist of a male dog and allows for more freedom of movement than a diaper. If a dog is experiencing both fecal and urinary accidents, a diaper is more appropriate. Changing diapers often enough to prevent skin infections and rashes is key. A barrier cream may also be helpful but try to find a cream that does not contain zinc oxide which is toxic if ingested. Some time each day without a diaper on can also help keep skin healthy.

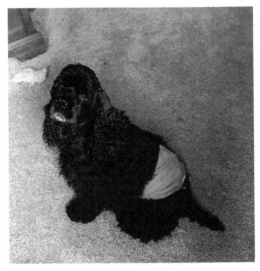

Belly band on Justice.

Finding ways to limit their access to absorbent surfaces, or pick bedding that is easily washed can make clean-ups easier. Waterproof pads or bedding are helpful. Watch your dog as well and see if you can identify 'tells' for when they need to go to the bathroom. For example, they may start to circle or sniff. Also give your dog more opportunities to go outside to relieve themself.

If your dog is becoming aggressive, fearful or anxious, you may need to keep them away from situations in which they could cause harm such as those involving other dogs or children.

Caring for a dog with CCD can be very demanding. It is so important to care for your own wellbeing as well and to take time for yourself. Seek out support from friends or online communities.

Other Causes

Other reasons for a change in your dog's behaviour as they get older are any disease or condition that can cause pain or discomfort. This includes dental disease, arthritis, cancer, muscle injury, ear infection and many others. If your dog's behaviour has suddenly changed it is best to take them into the vet for a check-up. Unaddressed pain can lead to aggression as the dog acts out to protect themself from unwanted touch.

Vision or hearing loss can increase anxiety making a dog more likely to act aggressively as well. With a loss of senses, it is easier to startle a dog and have them react negatively.

Tumours, hormone imbalances or any other condition that affects the brain can also change dog behaviour. Once again, this highlights the need for veterinarian examination if a dog is acting out of character.

~ 8 ~

Weight

It can feel like a personal attack when our veterinarian tells us that our dog is overweight. In the United States, it is estimated that 56% of dogs are overweight or obese.[32] Excess body weight can have a significantly negative effect on your dog; increased risk of cancers, arthritic changes, kidney dysfunction, diabetes, breathing difficulties and the list goes on. All of these can shorten the lifespan of your dog.

It is also important to keep in mind that not all extra weight means the same to all dogs. A small chihuahua who should weigh 6lbs and weighs 11lbs is overweight by 83% while a Great Dane who is 132lbs and overweight by the same 5lb amount is only overweight by 4%.

Determining if your Dog is at a Healthy Weight

Determining your dog's body condition score (BCS) can be more meaningful than the number on the scale when determining if your dog needs to lose weight. There are three things to look for when determining your dog's BCS:

1. *Waist* - looking down at your dog from above or running your hands over their sides if they are fluffy. Look and feel for an *hourglass* shape at the waist.

2. *Ribs* - run your hands over their ribcage. There should be minimal fat covering and you should be able to easily feel the ribs similar to if you ran your fingers over your knuckles with your hand open.

3. *Abdominal tuck* - Looking at your dog from the side and using your hands if needed. The abdomen should tuck upwards past the ribcage into the groin area.

From these findings, the dog is given a score between 1 and 9, where 1 is emaciated and 9 is obese. An ideal score is between 4 and 5.

Too Thin	1	*Ribs, spine, and hip bones are visible from a distance. No discernible body fat and an obvious loss of muscle mass.*	
	2	*Ribs, spine, and hip bones are easily visible. No palpable body fat and minimal loss of muscle mass.*	
	3	*Ribs can be easily felt and may be visible with no palpable fat. Top of the spine is visible and hip bones may also be prominent.*	
Ideal	4	*Ribs can be easily felt with minimal fat covering. Waist is easily noted when viewed from above. An "abdominal tuck" is also present, meaning that the abdomen appears tucked up behind the rib cage when viewed from the side.*	
	5	*Well-proportioned. Ribs can be easily felt without excess fat covering. Waist can be observed behind the ribs when viewed from above. Abdominal tuck is present.*	
Above Ideal	6	*Ribs can be felt through a slight excess fat covering. Waist is visible from above, but not prominent. Abdominal tuck is present.*	
Overweight	7	*Ribs are difficult to feel under a heavy fat covering. Noticeable fat deposits over the lower back and base of the tail. Waistline is absent or barely visible and the abdomen may appear obviously rounded or saggy.*	
	8	*Ribs can only be felt with heavy pressure. Significant fat deposits over the lower back and base of the tail. Waist and abdominal tuck are both absent. Obvious abdominal distention may also be present.*	
Obese	9	*Ribs cannot be felt under a very heavy fat covering. Large fat deposits are seen over the neck, chest, spine, and base of the tail. Waist and abdominal tuck are both absent. Obvious abdominal distention and a broad, flat back may also be present.*	

Weight Loss

Weight loss in dogs, like humans, requires a calorie deficit. More calories should be used up than are being consumed when trying to lose weight and typically this means less food being eaten and more movement.

When feeding your dog provide measured or weighed amounts of food so that you know how much they are getting. It is not advisable to free feed (i.e., putting out a bowl and letting them eat what they want) your dog when trying to help them lose weight.

If your dog does not seem satiated with the amount of food they are getting, you can use veggies as fillers. Examples include canned pumpkin (not pumpkin pie filling), carrots and green beans.

Cut back food in small amounts over time. For example, if you are feeding 1 cup for breakfast and dinner, start by cutting back by 1/8th of a cup each meal. Monitor your dog at this amount of food for a few weeks then re-assess if you need to cut back food again. If feeding a commercial dog food, keep in mind that the suggested calorie count on the bag if often overestimating your dog's needs! The more food your dog eats, the more money they make!

How many extras is your dog getting on a typical day? This includes treats and table scraps. It may be worth taking a few days to record on paper what these treats are amounting to. Many of us love our dogs with treats but we aren't doing them any favours health wise. If you are having trouble giving your dog fewer treats, there are other ways to minimize the impact. You can take a handful of kibbles from your measured meals to use as treats. Veggies are often appealing alternatives to traditional dog treats. You can also look for smaller sized dog treats (like training treats) or break larger treats into smaller pieces. Take a look at the back of the bag. For example, a large Dentastix contains 76kcal and the average 70lb dog needs 900-1050kcals/day[33]. One Dentastix is 7.7% of their daily calorie needs. More than one can really start to add up! Ingredients to avoid in treats are sugar, added fillers, animal by-product, chemicals and artificial preservatives. One alternative is to make your own treats at home to control what your dog gets.

Weight loss should also include an increase in activity if your dog is not getting enough. But do not add too much too quickly as this can lead to pain, a flare-up of arthritis or injuries. Consider adding an extra short walk to your routine or adding 5 minutes to an existing walk. Often what needs to be added are strengthening exercises, rather than more mileage, to build muscle. Short bouts of faster walking, such as between two driveways, can also help.

If all of your efforts seem to be in vain, consider discussing your dog's weight with your veterinarian. They can help to rule out any health issues that may be preventing your dog from losing weight such as a thyroid problem. They may also recommend a special dog food to help with weight control.

Keep in mind weight loss is usually a slow, gradual process. Be patient and consistent to see results. It's worth it!

Maggie at 78lbs   *Maggie at 63lbs*

~ 9 ~

Food and Nutrition

Changes in Appetite

A common complaint for owners of senior dogs is that their dog will suddenly not eat what they used to eat. Sometimes it doesn't need to be a worry. If your older dog has started to slow down and is not getting as much activity, they don't need as many calories. Metabolism also slows with age. So, if they are eating less, as opposed to not eating at all, consider if their activity level has also decreased and that may be the reason.

A more worrisome problem would be if they won't eat at all and aren't drinking. The risk of dehydration is serious. If your dog suddenly will not eat or drink, versus just being a picky eater, please see your veterinarian *immediately*. A senior dog who is dehydrated and has health issues can become very ill very quickly.

There may be some simple reasons why your dog may be refusing their meals or eating less. Is there anything that has changed recently that may be making them feel more stressed or anxious such as a move, a loss of a family member or a storm? Has your schedule changed or are you feeding them in a different spot? Have you changed their food or their food bowl recently? If you can identify a potential cause of anxiety, you may have found the reason they aren't eating.

Have you noticed your dog having more difficulty getting around? It is possible that they are having a hard time getting to their bowl to eat. Try making some changes to increase the ease of access to their food and see if that helps. Often a raised food and water bowl will make a big difference so that they don't have to reach down with their head and increase the weight through their front legs.

If you've ruled out some of the more benign reasons for a change in appetite and still cannot find an answer, it might be time for a trip to your veterinarian to have a check-up. They can help to rule in or out any medical issues that may be having an effect on their appetite.

Once you've seen your vet to rule out any serious reasons for your dog not wanting to eat, you can then start to try different things to get your dog eating again. Try adding some water to the bowl and warming it up in the microwave. This will make the food softer and also increase its smell. You could also try adding small amounts of human food to what you offer such as canned pumpkin, rice, carrots, broccoli, homemade bone broth or meats. Avoid salty, highly processed human foods. If you decide to change foods, do it gradually to limit the risk of an upset stomach. It can be tricky at times to know if your dog is acting a certain way to get the foods they desire more (i.e., human foods over their same old boring dog food). There is no easy answer to this, especially for a stubborn dog who will wait you out until you give in and offer what you know they will eat!

Senior Dog Food

As discussed in Chapter 1, because there is no defined age at which all dogs become a senior, it is difficult to point to an age at which all dogs may need to switch to a "senior" dog food, if at all. There are some helpful things to keep in mind when determining what to feed your senior dog:

Protein. Lower amounts of dietary protein can lead to muscle loss in dogs. Research suggests that healthy older dogs could benefit from a higher protein to calorie ratio with at least 25% of the calories coming from protein.[34]

Body Condition Score. If your dog is overweight or obese (see chapter 8), then you may need to reduce the calorie and fat content in your dog's diet.

Chronic Health Conditions. Dogs with osteoarthritis may benefit from nutrients in food that reduce inflammation, such as fatty acids. Decreasing dietary phosphorus can be beneficial in dogs with kidney disease.[35] Reducing sodium intake can be beneficial for dogs with kidney disease,[36] heart disease or high blood pressure.[37]

If your dog is of good health, at an ideal weight and is eating a balanced diet, there is likely no need to change your dog's food as they age. It is very important to ensure you are making decisions made with science versus those based on marketing. One option to ensure you are getting reliable, educated nutrition advice is to work with a Board Certified Veterinary Nutritionist (US) or a Clinical Nutrition Service (Canada). These veterinarians have specialized training in canine nutrition and can help you ensure your dog is getting the best nutrition for their specific needs.

Joint Supplements

Perform a Google search for "dog joint supplements" and you can quickly become overwhelmed. There are many different products on the market and each vet and dog food store seems to have their own opinion about what the best choice is for your dog. Not only can you give your dog a canine-specific supplement, you can also buy dog food that is formulated for joint health, or give them human-grade supplements. How does one decide?! There is no one size fits all for every dog but there are some guidelines to follow:

1. Use the **ACCLAIM** method to help determine safety of a product:

   A = **A** name you recognize.

   C = **C**linical experience. A company who participates in clinical trials to ensure safety and efficacy of a product.

   C = **C**ontents. All ingredients and amounts should be clearly stated on the label.

   L = **L**abel claims. If they sound too good to be true, they probably are. Claims of "curing" or "preventing" should be treated as suspect.

A = **A**dministration recommendations. The dosage should be easy to calculate for the size of your dog.

I = **I**dentification of lot number. This indicates that there is a quality control method and allows for recall of a product if needed.

M = **M**anufacturer information. You should be able to easily identify where the product was made and by whom.

2. Look for ingredients that have been shown by research to help manage arthritis.

   i. Glucosamine[38] - it may take 2-3 months to have an effect. It is also suggested that the dosage is higher when starting to give your dog this supplement and then the dosage can be decreased to a maintenance dose. Dosage is best discussed with your veterinarian.

   ii. Omega-3 Fatty Acids[39] - 50-220mg/kg is suggested as a dosage guideline.[40] EPA and DHA are common sources of Omega-3 fatty acids.

   iii. Chondroitin Sulfate - May be beneficial when taken with glucosamine at a dosage of 15-30mg/kg[41]

   iv. Green lipped mussel extract[42] - There are no standard dosage guidelines. Effectiveness has been shown to be similar with use of a powder, treat or when incorporated into food.[43]

Another good question is when should you start giving your dog a joint supplement? Again, there are no standardized answers but there are a few key things to consider:

Start early. Some sources will suggest that you should start giving your dog a joint supplement as soon as they reach 1 year old. The reasoning is that many dogs have osteoarthritic changes in the joint before any signs and symptoms are seen by the owner or veterinarian. This is a choice every owner should consider. It may be prudent to start a joint supplement once your dog starts to show any signs of aging.

Your dog has had a joint injury or surgery. If your dog has had an injury such as an injury to a muscle, tendon or bone, the risk of developing osteoarthritis increases.[44] This is believed to be caused by the inflammation that happens with an injury. Joint surgeries also significantly increase the risk of osteoarthritis occurring at that joint.[45]

When selecting a joint supplement for your dog, consider these recommendations to make the best choice for the needs of your won dog.

~ 10 ~

Exercise

Exercise is important at any age but often tends to become a bit more anxiety provoking for owners of senior dogs. There is a fear of hurting their dog. How do you know if you are doing too much or not enough?

Walking is probably the most common form of exercise for most dogs. It is usually pretty simple for both dog and owner to manage a walk together. With an older dog a walk may need to be modified. For example, if you are used to walking your dog for 30-minutes without a rest break once a day but now your dog is struggling to keep up with this consider breaking the walk into shorter walks. This could mean going out for two 15-minute walks instead. Or it could be a walk of 20-minutes, stopping and resting at a park bench for 10-minutes then continuing the last 10-minutes to get back home. Your dog should not be any lamer at the end of a walk than when they started out. If they are, the walk may have been too long. Other signs you have pushed your dog too much on a walk are:

- Lying down and refusing to continue walking

- Stumbling, tripping or falling

- Dragging of limbs (listen for nails scraping concrete or asphalt)

We must also remember to be smarter than our dogs. It can be tempting to allow our dogs to do more than their normal amount of exercise because they are continuing to do it. Don't let them fool you! This can set your dog up for pain and injury. Again, owning a dog is much like parenting a young child - if we let them do whatever they want, sooner or later they are going to get hurt. The risk of doing this with an older dog is that they do not 'bounce back' like a younger dog. Use some of the following strategies to help manage a dog that tends to overdo it. Maybe they need to be kept on a leash to avoid them running around with too much enthusiasm. Limit their play areas if they tend to get going wildly in an open area. This could mean putting your dog in a crate if they tend to get out of hand with other dogs in your home when you are out. Set a time limit for exercise, whether it be for a walk or for play time.

Throwing a ball is another typical dog activity that can lead to much greater harm with an older dog. If your dog is really struggling with walking, consider this activity banned for your dog. If your senior dog is still strong and playful and you wish to still toss the ball for them, do so with precautions. Start out with a warm-up (discussed below). Then make it a boring game. Your tosses should be low to the ground, predictable (i.e., the ball isn't bouncing from one direction to the other) and on a stable surface (i.e., no wet grass!). One way to continue to play ball or frisbee is to have your dog run to a ball/frisbee that doesn't move once it hits the ground. You should also limit the number of throws. Again, your dog may want and be willing to do 10, 50 or 100 fetches, but you need to know better. A good limit might be 3 to 5 throws. Then offer a cool-down.

Warm-up and Cool-Down

A warm-up and cool-down should be completed as often as you are doing any other physical activity. If you are exercising your dog more than once a day that means you should be warming-up and cooling down your dog each time.

The purpose of a warm-up is to prepare your dog's body for increased workloads and reduce the risk of injury. The purpose of a cool-down is to calm and relax your dog after activity, allowing their muscles to return to their lengthened state while removing lactic acid. Cooling-down reduces the risk of chronically tight muscles and returns the heart rate back to resting levels.

The need for a warm-up or cool-down on a daily walk may depend on the weather. If the temperature is cool or cold and the conditions are slippery, a proper warm-up is key to preparing the body for the elements and ensuring the dog is prepared if they slip. If the temperatures are warm, a cool-down is more important to help ensure your dog's body temperature is decreasing slowly and the heart is relaxing gradually. In more moderate temperatures, there is greater ability to warm-up on the go. Start the walk slowly and then gradually build to your walking pace. As you get closer to the end of your walk, likewise slow down your pace.

If you are doing an activity that is more intense than a neighbourhood stroll (e.g., hiking, swimming) or the temperatures are not conducive to a warm-up or cool-down on the go, the warm-up and cool-down may need to be more involved.

Warm-up. A warm-up should be 5-10 minutes in length - longer for activities of greater intensity. No equipment is required for a warm-up and you should not work your dog to fatigue. Pick dynamic movements (i.e., not standing still) that mimic the activity you are going to be doing with your dog. You should avoid static stretching (i.e., holding a position for longer than a few seconds) in the warm-up. When static stretching is done during a warm-up it can actually make it easier for your dog to get hurt. Static stretching reduces maximum muscle forces and decreases jumping height, run speed, balance and reaction time, though in many senior dogs we are not concerned about speed and jumping unless we have dogs that are still engaged in this type of high intensity activity.

A warm-up could begin with 2-3 minutes light trotting followed by:

- Circles in each direction
- Sit to stands
- Play-bows

Play bow. Note: Position should not be held in a warm-up.
Your dog should stand back up again after elbows touch the ground.

- Cookies to the hip

Cookies to hip. Note: Position should not be held in a warm-up.

- Activity specific warm-up (such as before agility, fetch)
  - low jumps
  - active heeling
  - weave between legs
  - catching a ball thrown into a corner

Cool-down. The cool-down should be just as long as the warm-up and may include the same activities as your warm-up but with less intensity and fewer repetitions. Static stretching is appropriate during the cool-down. Especially in hot or warm environments, your cool-down may include a means of decreasing your dog's body temperature such as a cooling pad or water. In cold environments, be mindful that the body isn't losing heat too quickly which can increase lactic acid retention and muscle cramping/discomfort. If the temperatures are cold and your cool-down is outdoors, consider lengthening your cool-down.

Your cool-down should begin and end with walking with stretching in the middle. You do not need to repeat the activity specific components you did in your warm-up. Stretches should be gentle, meaning the position to hold is where you feel resistance to moving the limb further. Stretches held for 15 to 30 seconds may include:

- Bicep stretch. With your dog relaxed, gently flex the shoulder and extend the elbow towards the tail.

- Triceps stretch. With your dog relaxed, gently extend the shoulder and elbow towards the nose

- Hip flexor stretch. With your dog relaxed, gentle extend the hip and leg towards the tail.

Senior Dog Strength Exercises

Strength exercises done 3 days a week, for 5-10 minutes can be an excellent complement to your walking routine. If you are unsure of how to adjust the following exercises for your dog, it is suggested you work with a canine exercise professional to avoid causing your dog injury. Watch for signs of fatigue when exercising your dog. These include, yawning and panting, losing interest in the activity, muscles shaking or quivering and loss of good form. Watch your dog's posture – if they start to arch or round their back, splay their feet or have difficulty keeping their knees and elbows under them, they may be tired. If your dog starts to fatigue, give them a rest break or discontinue the exercise session. It is often better to do too little and avoid injury than to push your dog too hard.

Plank. Many senior dogs lack abdominal/core strength and stand with their back feet too far forward. In this exercise, have your dog stand with front feet under their shoulders then move one rearfoot at a time backwards so that they have to use more of their core muscles to support themself. The ultimate goal is for the hocks (lower part of the back leg) to be perpendicular to the ground. Hold this position for 3-5 seconds then release your dog (i.e., let them move). Repeat 5 times.

As your dog gains more strength you will be able to further slide the rear feet back until you reach the ideal plank (i.e., stacked) position.

Poor positioning. Maggie's back legs are forward and her front lets are not perpendicular to the ground.

Ideal plank posture. Note the treat placement is a little high. Ideally the head should be straight ahead.

Squats. Similar to a human squat, this exercise works on hind end strength and flexibility of the hip and knee. The aim is to have the dog slowly sit into a square sit and then slowly stand up. This is similar to a squat a human would perform. This exercise can be made easier by having your dog sit onto a raised step or helping to guide their backend down so that they sit squarely. It can be made more challenging by asking your dog to stand back up just before their bum touches the floor or by having their front limbs on an elevated platform or have them standing on an unstable surface like a couch cushion. Having the dog sit down while facing up a hill will also increase the challenge on the back end. Aim for 5-10 repetitions and watch for fatigue.

**if your dog is coming from a show/obedience background we are not looking for a kick back stand

*Dog squat. We used an aerobics step covered with a towel
to help Maggie sit with her legs close to her body.*

Push-ups. This exercise challenges the strength and flexibility of the shoulder and upper back. The aim is for your dog to lower its weight onto its elbows and then push up. This is similar to a human push-up. When your dog is in the push-up position the elbows should be bent at 90 degrees under the shoulders. Your dog's bum should remain in the air. This exercise can be made easier by encouraging them to bend their elbows and lower towards the floor even if they are unable to touch their elbows to the floor. If your dog does not understand what you want them to do, try luring them with a treat under your outstretched leg. Aim for 5-10 repetitions and watch for fatigue.

Dog Push-up. If your dog does not know the command "bow" or will not lower their front end following a lure, you can encourage them under an outstretched leg

Cookies to the hip. This is a great exercise to work on spine flexibility and core strength. Stand at your dog's side on the opposite side you want your dog to turn to. Take a treat from their nose slowly back towards their hip and reward them. If your dog is very stiff/arthritic in their back, they may not be able to bring their nose all the way back and that is okay. Work within your dog's limits. Aim for 5-10 repetitions on each side.

Happy Doggie Bum Rub. This is a great way to get your dog to contract the muscles in their back legs and put more weight through their back legs. All you need to do is scratch your dog's bum! They will often push their rump into your hand for more!

Feet up. The purpose of this exercise is to increase weight bearing through the back legs in order to strengthen them. This can be done on the bottom step facing the stairs or on an aerobics platform. Your dog's front feet are on the step and their nose is lured upwards to shift their body weight into their back legs (otherwise the weight is more in their front legs). It can easily be made harder or easier by changing the height of the step. Aim for your dog to stay in this position for 5-10 seconds and repeat 5 times.

If your dog is struggling even on a small platform, practice the plank exercise for a few weeks before progressing to this exercise until your dog can hold a plank for 10 seconds.

Feet up exercise on the bottom stair.

Ladder walking. You can use an extension ladder laid down on the ground, or you can make one out of pool noodles and paracord. Start by walking your dog forward through the rungs. This task can be made harder by simply going faster. To increase the challenge, you could also have your dog move backwards through the ladder or sideways through the ladder with just their front or back feet. You could also put the ladder on an unstable surface (foam) or on an incline. Aim for a few passes through on whatever level of challenge your dog is ready for.

Ladder walking through a pool noodle.

Exercise

Walking Backwards. When first trying this exercise with your dog, try walking your dog forward between two objects, such as the couch and coffee table, and then walk towards your dog giving the command 'back-up'. Practicing between two objects will help prevent your dog from turning around and walking forwards. This can be made harder by changing the surface the dog walks on (e.g., on a foam pad) or having them walk backwards over objects (e.g., broom stick, pool noodles, etc.). Aim for up to 5 passes.

~ 11 ~

Enrichment

When our senior dogs start to slow down or have more trouble walking, it is easy to forget about the importance of still going out in the world and the benefit it can have on their mental health. Consider how you start to feel if you are stuck in the house for several days due to poor weather. Do you start to feel tired, unmotivated and foggy? Our dogs can experience the same thing.

There are four areas in which we can provide enrichment opportunities for our dog: cognitive/mental, sensory, social/play and physical.

Cognitive/mental enrichment includes many of the things we may already be doing with our dogs such as puzzle toys and slow feeder bowls. These activities challenge your dog's thinking and problem-solving skills. Other ways to engage your dog in cognitive enrichment could be basic training and trick training. Consider working with a certified dog trainer if you need assistance in training your dog. Puzzle toys are vastly available in most pet stores. Consider the level of challenge your dog needs as some are more complicated than others. You can also create DIY puzzle toys. Examples include using a muffin tin with treats in the cups covered by tennis balls so the dog has to remove the balls or hiding treats in a cereal box filed with crumpled newspaper and your dog needs to get to the treats.

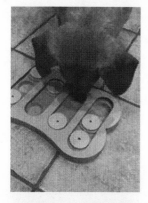

Napoleon working on a puzzle toy.

Elphaba looking for treats hidden in a blanket in a bin.

Sensory enrichment involves engaging your dog in activities typical to their species (i.e., dogs doing dog things!) such as chewing, digging, foraging and tugging. Providing your dog with opportunities to chew on safe, appropriate objects can be really beneficial for a dog. Many of us get irritated with a dog who tears apart a stuffed dog toy but it is normal behaviour for a dog. Instead of getting frustrated, save the stuffing from the toy and make a second toy in an old sock. If they like to dig, provide your dog with an appropriate spot to dig such as a spot in your yard (if you are up for it!) or take them to a sandy beach. Foraging or looking for food can be done with a snuffle mat or scattering food in the grass. Breed specific games can also provide enrichment. Retrievers are bred to retrieve so a short, safe game of fetch might light them up. Border collies and cattle dogs herd. Be creative and try to come up with ability appropriate variations to encourage these natural behaviours.

It also may be a time to allow them a little more freedom on your walks to 'smell the roses.' A decompression walk, or "sniffari", in which a dog is allowed to go at their own pace, and freedom to move and sniff has been shown to be very relaxing for a dog and have a positive impact on their mental well-being.

Social or play enrichment might be achieved by letting your dog visit with other dogs that might be more on the boring side (aka not wanting to wrestle). It could also be playing with you. Social enrichment can be more relaxed, such as letting your dog visit with other people you pass on walks, neighbours or other family members. It could be just spending time together, such as them sitting with you quietly while you read.

Physical enrichment really encompasses any physical activity or exercise you engage your dog in. Any of the exercises we discussed in chapter 10 would fit this category as well as swimming, hiking and anything else that gets your dog moving.

We discussed in chapter 7 the benefit of sunshine and light exposure for dogs with cognitive decline. But what else can we do besides that? We can go for a ride in the car. We can use a wagon or stroller to take the dog for a 'walk'. For smaller dogs, you may be able to tote them along in a backpack. This can help with all categories of enrichment.

Gerard enjoying a walk in his dog stroller.

~ 12 ~

Nail Care

Keeping our dog's nails short and the hair between their toe pads trimmed can have a big impact at any age, but especially when our dogs are older. Long nails change the posture of a dog just like wearing high heels can change our posture.

A dog gets balance from the floor by being able to spread out their paw pads. In order for a dog to be able to get their footpads on the floor when their nails are too long, they will stand with their weight backwards instead of over top of their paws. Imagine this: a dog with long nails will stand with their front and back legs closer together and their back rounded. Cu their nails shorter and their back will flatten and their front and back feet will be farther apart.

Boss's long nails are causing him to shift his weight backwards. Notice his front legs are angled forward.

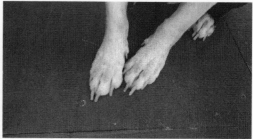

It can be a daunting task to cut a dog's nails and even more so if the nails are very long or black. If you aren't used to cutting your dog's nails it is best done slowly, possibly only doing a few nails at a time. Provide lots of praise and maybe some treats! If your dog's nails are really long, don't expect to get them trimmed down to an ideal length anytime soon. As a nail grows longer, the quick (aka blood supply of the nail) also grows longer. As the nail is gradually shortened every few weeks, the quick will recede. Ideally, the nails should be short enough that you do not hear them clicking on hard floors.

You may find that different styles of nail trimmers work better for you and your dog than others. Guillotine-type clippers in which the nail it placed in a hole and then squeezed to clip the nail, are best for small to medium sized dogs. A scissor-type nail clipper is better for larger dogs with stronger nails as the guillotine may not cut through their nails. These function as the name implies, like scissors. Both types of clippers run the risk of cutting too much off of the nail and cutting the quick. Alternatively, a dremel is a grinding tool that wears down a dog's nail with friction. It may be easier to avoid the quick with a dremel but it can still happen. Some dogs are also anxious about the noise the dremel makes.

If you are anxious about trimming your dog's nails, as many dog owners are, it is money well spent to have someone else cut them for you.

Another easy way to give your senior dog a leg up is to trim the fur between the toe pads. If the fur between the toe pads starts to grow over the foot pads this can be very slippery. Compare this to running down a tile hallway with socks on versus running shoes. Toe fur can be easily trimmed with a pair of sharp scissors.

~ 13 ~

Home Modifications

There are lots of things we can adjust in our homes to make life easier for our older dogs. Oftentimes you can use something you already have on hand to make some changes for your dog, or you can buy products specifically made for your needs.

Elevated food bowls. Raising up the food bowl can keep your dog from having to flex their necks and back towards the ground to eat. Using a platform for their bowls will also lighten the pressure through their front legs which can be very helpful if they have sore, arthritic joints. You can purchase raised bowl platforms or use household objects like a shoe box or a step stool. To determine if the bowls are high enough watch your dog eat. The top of the food bowl should be at approximately the same height as their lower chest so they don't have to lower their head.

Boss using a box to raise up his food bowl.

Flooring. What is the flooring in your home like? If it is carpeted, great! If you have tile, hardwood or laminate consider putting down area rugs, runners or even yoga mats to help keep your dog from slipping. Not only will this help keep your dog confidently moving around your home, it can help prevent injuries. Try to target areas where they frequently walk and turn. Don't forget about slippery stairs.

Bedding. Arthritic joints can be tender to lie on. Provide your dog with a soft place to rest that cushions their body. Be mindful of not giving them an overly cushioned spot, as that can be difficult for a dog to balance on if they have weakness or mobility issues.

Temperature. Older dogs can have more difficulty regulating their temperature and are more sensitive to temperatures that vary greatly from their own (i.e., too hot or too cold). A thermostat set to 20 to 23 degrees Celsius (or 68 to 73 degrees Fahrenheit) is ideal. Try to avoid having your dog's bed in a drafty spot.

Stairs/Ramp. Does your dog like to get up onto the couch or your bed? If so, you can provide them with stairs to get up. You can buy a set of stairs specifically made for your pet, or you can improvise and make your own with sturdy objects like an aerobic step. You can also consider a ramp instead of steps. Don't be surprised if they don't use it right away. It may take a bit of training to get them used to it. Try luring them with a treat and lots of praise if they use what you've supplied them with.

Earl using his ramp to get outside.

Smells. If your dog has lost their vision, one way to help them find their way around the home is to diffuse different smells in different rooms. This can help your dog learn where they are in the house depending on the scent you use. Be sure to use a high-quality essential oils brand (like Doterra) to avoid adding toxins to your home and place the diffuser in a place that your dog cannot knock it over or drink the water.

~ 14 ~

Equipment that can help

Harness to help lift or support can help both you and your dog. If your dog is having difficulty getting up from lying, needs support on the stairs or is wobbly or weak, a special harness can keep your dog active and using their legs while saving your back from having to lean over to hold them up.

Napoleon getting some hind end support from a sling after back surgery for IVDD.

The Help 'Em Up Harness[46] is a popular option and is designed to be worn by your dog throughout the day so you don't have to take it on and off like other slings. It evenly distributes the weight through the harness and provides the owner with handles to support the dog.

Winston wearing his Help'Em Up Harness.

There are many other brands of support harnesses commercially available. An owner can also create their own sling with a fabric tote back by cutting out the side panels or using a towel for support under a dog's abdomen.

Booties or toe grips provide an alternative to covering slippery floors, especially if your dog seeks out spots to lie down where there is no carpet. Without traction between the nail and the floor, a dog can have increased difficulty getting up from the floor, or can lose their balance.

Dr. Buzby's ToeGrips[47] are rubber, non-slip nail grips that fit over a dog's nail to provide traction. ToeGrips will not work if your dog's toenails don't touch the floor, because the rubber grip will also not touch the floor.

Beau wearing green toe grips.

Booties or grip socks can also increase traction as well. Some dogs will adopt a very strange walking pattern with boots on. If your dog does not acclimatize to wearing boots it's best to try a different style or solution.

Dog strollers or bike carriers can help you continue to get your dog outside. There are strollers and carriers specially made for dogs. Some are even equipped with safety harnesses! Ensure that you get one that can accommodate the size and weight of your dog comfortably. If your dog is unable to relax or tries to escape while on the move, you may need to do some training with your dog in the stroller while it is not moving. A jump from a height could significantly injure your dog.

Lily meeting up with friends in her dog stroller.

Dog ramps and stairs (as discussed in chapter 13) are very beneficial in preventing your dog from jumping up or down off of high surfaces. You can purchase portable dog ramps that can be used for your vehicle or other areas or you can build your own if you have the skills. If using a ramp, look for one that provides some traction for your dog's paws.

Dog Wheelchairs are beneficial for dogs whose back legs don't work well but the rest of their body is healthy. It can provide a dog with more independence than a support sling, as the dog can then walk and go to the bathroom independently. A wheelchair is not meant to be used at all times since the dog cannot lie down in it. It is recommended to work with a dog care professional to ensure proper wheelchair fit and use.

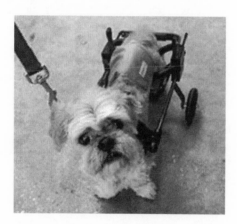

Rocky in his wheelchair.

~ 15 ~

When is it Time to Say Goodbye?

From the day we get our dog, whether it be as an 8-week-old puppy or as a rehomed dog at 12 years old, we know in the back of our minds that we will probably reach the point of having to make the final decision about when to say goodbye. Every owner fears making the wrong decision and doing it sooner than they need to. Every second seems valuable when nearing the end of the life of a good friend.

It's an emotional and very difficult decision to make. It is important to speak to those you trust about your thoughts and feelings. That could be a spouse or other family members, friends or anyone else who has worked with you and your dog.

When we make the decision to release our dogs from this world and a failing body there may be comfort in making that decision and that is okay. There is often guilt and that is normal. We are gently allowing them to leave this world and allowing them to pass in the best way that we know how. We are also making sure that they are not alone as they pass. It is a final opportunity to be with them and to let them know they are loved and cared for.

HHHHHMMM Scale by Dr. Alice Villalobos[48]

There is no black and white answer about when the right time for your dog to cross over is but there are tools that can help you decide what your dog's quality of life is like. Living is about so much more than "being alive". Your dog's quality of life is more to do with how they feel about their life than it is about living.

A commonly used tool to determine your dog's quality of life is the *HHHHHMM Scale* by Dr. Alice Villalobos. You can access the full scale at https://www.veterinarypracticenews.com/quality-of-life-scale/.

For each item, score your dog from 1 (poor) to 10 (best). A score of 35 or less would be considered an unacceptable quality of life.

Hurt /10	Is the patient in pain, including distress from difficulty in breathing? Can the pet's pain be successfully managed? Is oxygen necessary?
Hunger /10	Is the pet eating enough? Does hand-feeding help? Does the pet require a feeding tube?
Hydration /10	Is the pet dehydrated? Are subcutaneous fluids once or twice daily enough to resolve the problem? Are they well tolerated?
Hygiene /10	The pet should be kept brushed and clean, particularly after elimination. Does the pet have pressure sores?
Happiness /10	Does the pet express joy and interest? Is he responsive to things around him (family, toys, etc)? Is the pet depressed, lonely, anxious, bored, or afraid? Can the pet's bed be near the kitchen and moved near family activities to minimize isolation?
Mobility /10	Can the pet get up without assistance? Does the pet need human or mechanical help (e.g., a cart)? Does she feel like going for a walk? Is she having seizures or stumbling? Note: Some caregivers feel euthanasia is preferable to amputation, yet an animal with limited mobility may still be alert and responsive, and can have a good quality of life as long as the family is committed to quality care.
More Good Days than Bad /10	When bad days outnumber good days, the pet's suffering is appreciable and quality of life might be too compromised. When a healthy human-animal bond is no longer possible, the caregiver must be made aware that the end is near.

There are veterinarians that specialize in end-of-life care for pets. They have specialized training and can offer unique skills and support during a very difficult time. They usually provide these services in your own home which can provide an added level of comfort for you and your dog.

Cherish the Memories

"Just this side of heaven is a place called Rainbow Bridge.

When an animal dies that has been especially close to someone here, that pet goes to Rainbow Bridge. There are meadows and hills for all of our special friends so they can run and play together. There is plenty of food, water and sunshine, and our friends are warm and comfortable.

All the animals who had been ill and old are restored to health and vigor. Those who were hurt or maimed are made whole and strong again, just as we remember them in our dreams of days and times gone by. The animals are happy and content, except for one small thing; they each miss someone very special to them, who had to be left behind.

They all run and play together, but the day comes when one suddenly stops and looks into the distance. His bright eyes are intent. His eager body quivers. Suddenly he begins to run from the group, flying over the green grass, his legs carrying him faster and faster.

You have been spotted, and when you and your special friend finally meet, you cling together in joyous reunion, never to be parted again. The happy kisses rain upon your face; your hands again caress the beloved head, and you look once more into the trusting eyes of your pet, so long gone from your life but never absent from your heart.

Then you cross Rainbow Bridge together...."

— Author unknown

Shades with a rainbow.

Depending on where you live, there are different options for your dog's body after they have passed, whether it be burial or cremation. These are best discussed with your veterinarian.

Beyond the loss of their physical body, it can be very healing to create a memory of your pet. Listed below are some options. There is no wrong way to memorialize your family member that has passed.

1. Urns

2. Headstones

3. Photo Albums or Books

4. Jewellery

5. Special Area Dedicated to Them in Your Home

6. Paw Print Mould

Sweet Neutron is remembered by his mom Kathy

What Did You Think of *This Old Dog*?

First of all, thank you for purchasing this book. I know you could have picked any number of books about senior dogs, but you picked this book and for that I am extremely grateful.

I hope that you found it to be a useful tool for caring for your older dog and that is adds value and quality to your dog's everyday life. If so, it would be really nice if you could share this book with your friends and family by posting to Facebook and Twitter.

If you enjoyed this book and found some benefit in reading this, I'd like to hear from you and hope that you could take some time to post a review on Amazon. Your feedback and support will help other owners with their senior dogs.

You can leave a review for This Old Dog by putting this link into your internet browser:

Amazon.com/review/create-review?&asin=B08QXH41MG

I want you, the reader, to know that your review is very important and so, if you'd like to leave a review, all you have to do is go to the website above, or search for This Old Dog on Amazon.

I wish you and your dog many more days together!

About the Author

Shauna Slobodian is a registered physiotherapist and canine rehab therapist in Kingston, Ontario, Canada. She graduated from Queen's University with a Master of Science in Physical Therapy degree in 2010 and has a Diploma in Canine Rehabilitation through the Animal Rehab Division of the Canadian Physiotherapy Association.

Shauna is the owner of Pawsitively Fit Canine Rehabilitation & Wellness where the mission is to *help healthy senior dogs stay active, without pain, so that they can have more days with their owners to do the things they love!* Her experience working with senior dogs shines through in *This Old Dog*.

After years of working with seniors of the human variety, Shauna realized she was seeing the same thing with seniors of the four-legged kind. Often seniors were being overlooked and not provided with the education and tools they needed to maximize the quality of their later years. That's why, in 2019, Shauna decided to focus Pawsitively Fit on helping senior dogs. They had too much to gain to continue to allow them to be overlooked.

Shauna is also active in advocating for the role of physiotherapists as the provider of choice for canine rehabilitation. She is a member of the executive committee of the Animal Rehab Division of the Canadian Physiotherapy Association. She also manages the Facebook Group *Our Healthy Senior Dogs,* which is an online community for sharing advice and stories between owners of senior dogs.

You can connect with Shauna on Social Media:

Our Healthy Senior Dogs Facebook Group
www.facebook.com/groups/ourhealthyseniordogs

Facebook **@pawsitivelyfitkingston**

Instagram **@pawsitively_fit**

Website **www.pawsitivelyfit.ca**

References

[1] Hiscox, L. & Bellows, J. (n.d.). *Dental Disease in Dogs*. VCA Hospitals. https://vcahospitals.com/know-your-pet/dental-disease-in-dogs

[2] Conzemius, M. G., & Evans, R. B. (2012). Caregiver placebo effect for dogs with lameness from osteoarthritis. *Journal of the American Veterinary Medical Association, 241*(10), 1314–1319. https://doi.org/10.2460/javma.241.10.1314

[3] Malek, S., Sample, S. J., Schwartz, Z., Nemke, B., Jacobson, P. B., Cozzi, E. M., Schaefer, S. L., Bleedorn, J. A., Holzman, G., & Muir, P. (2012). Effect of analgesic therapy on clinical outcome measures in a randomized controlled trial using client-owned dogs with hip osteoarthritis. *BMC veterinary research, 8*, 185. https://doi.org/10.1186/1746-6148-8-185

[4] Canine Arthritis Management. (n.d.). *Arthritis - The Basics*. https://caninearthritis.co.uk/what-is-arthritis/

[5] Dictionary.com. (n.d.). *Degenerate*. https://www.dictionary.com/browse/degenerate?s=t

[6] Goldring M. B. (2006). Update on the biology of the chondrocyte and new approaches to treating cartilage diseases. *Best practice & research. Clinical rheumatology, 20*(5), 1003–1025. https://doi.org/10.1016/j.berh.2006.06.003

[7] Edge-Hughes, L. (2020, May 9). *Reversing Osteoarthritis*. Four Leg Rehab Inc - Laurie's Blog. https://www.fourleg.com/Blog?b=460

[8] Anderson, K. L., O'Neill, D. G., Brodbelt, D. C., Church, D. B., Meeson, R. L., Sargan, D., Summers, J. F., Zulch, H., & Collins, L. M. (2018). Prevalence, duration and risk factors for appendicular osteoarthritis in a UK dog population under primary veterinary care. *Scientific reports, 8*(1), 5641. https://doi.org/10.1038/s41598-018-23940-z

[9] Innes, J. F., Clayton, J., & Lascelles, B. D. (2010). Review of the safety and efficacy of long-term NSAID use in the treatment of canine osteoarthritis. *The Veterinary record, 166*(8), 226–230. https://doi.org/10.1136/vr.c97

[10] Monteiro-Steagall, B P et al. "Systematic review of nonsteroidal anti-inflammatory drug-induced adverse effects in dogs." *Journal of veterinary internal medicine* vol. 27,5 (2013): 1011-9. doi:10.1111/jvim.12127

[11] Robertson, S.A. (2008). *Monitoring Dogs on NSAIDS*. Clinician's Brief. https://www.cliniciansbrief.com/article/monitoring-dogs-nsaids

[12] Churchill, Julie. (2018, May 3-5). *The Fountain of Age: Feeding Strategies for Senior Pets*. [Conference Session]. Companion Animal Nutrition Summit. Charleston, South Carolina.

[13] Adams, V. J., Evans, K. M., Sampson, J., & Wood, J. L. (2010). Methods and mortality results of a health survey of purebred dogs in the UK. *The Journal of small animal practice, 51*(10), 512–524. https://doi.org/10.1111/j.1748-5827.2010.00974.x

[14] Vail, D. M., & MacEwen, E. G. (2000). Spontaneously occurring tumors of companion animals as models for human cancer. *Cancer investigation, 18*(8), 781–792. https://doi.org/10.3109/07357900009012210.

[15] Animal Cancer Foundation. (n.d). *Cancer Education.* http://acfoundation.org/cancer-education/

[16] Morello, E., Martano, M., & Buracco, P. (2011). Biology, diagnosis and treatment of canine appendicular osteosarcoma: similarities and differences with human osteosarcoma. *Veterinary journal (London, England: 1997), 189*(3), 268–277. https://doi.org/10.1016/j.tvjl.2010.08.014

[17] Anfinsen, K. P., Grotmol, T., Bruland, O. S., & Jonasdottir, T. J. (2011). Breed-specific incidence rates of canine primary bone tumors--a population-based survey of dogs in Norway. *Canadian journal of veterinary research = Revue Canadienne de recherche veterinaire, 75*(3), 209–215.

[18] Sapierzyński, R., & Czopowicz, M. (2017). The animal-dependent risk factors in canine osteosarcomas. *Polish journal of veterinary sciences, 20*(2), 293–298. https://doi.org/10.1515/pjvs-2017-0035

[19] Withrow, S.J., Vail, D., & Page, R. (2013). *Withrow & MacEwen's Small Animal Clinical Oncology.* (D. Vail, Ed). Elsevier.

[20] Straw, R. C., Withrow, S. J., Richter, S. L., Powers, B. E., Klein, M. K., Postorino, N. C., LaRue, S. M., Ogilvie, G. K., Vail, D. M., & Morrison, W. B. (1991). Amputation and cisplatin for treatment of canine osteosarcoma. *Journal of veterinary internal medicine, 5*(4), 205–210. https://doi.org/10.1111/j.1939-1676.1991.tb00950.x

[21] Culp, W. T., Olea-Popelka, F., Sefton, J., Aldridge, C. F., Withrow, S. J., Lafferty, M. H., Rebhun, R. B., Kent, M. S., & Ehrhart, N. (2014). Evaluation of outcome and prognostic factors for dogs living greater than one year after diagnosis of osteosarcoma: 90 cases (1997-2008). *Journal of the American Veterinary Medical Association, 245*(10), 1141–1146. https://doi.org/10.2460/javma.245.10.1141

[22] Holt, P. E. (1985) Urinary Incontinence in the Bitch Due to Sphincter Mechanism Incompetence: Prevalence in Referred Dogs and Retrospective Analysis of Sixty Cases. *Journal of Small Animal Practice.* 26(4), 181–190. doi:10.1111/j.1748-5827.1985.tb02099.x.

[23] Arnold S. (1997). Harninkontinenz bei kastrierten Hündinnen. Teil 1: Bedeutung, Klinik und Atiopathogenese [Urinary incontinence in castrated bitches. Part 1: Significance, clinical aspects and etiopathogenesis]. *Schweizer Archiv für Tierheilkunde, 139*(6), 271–276.

[24] Coit, V. A., Gibson, I. F., Evans, N. P., & Dowell, F. J. (2008). Neutering affects urinary bladder function by different mechanisms in male and female dogs.

European journal of pharmacology, 584(1), 153–158.
https://doi.org/10.1016/j.ejphar.2008.02.037

[25] Morgan, J.P., Hansson, K. and Miyabayashi, T. (1989). Spondylosis deformans in the female beagle dog: A radiographic study. *Journal of Small Animal Practice*, 30, 457-460. https://doi.org/10.1111/j.1748-5827.1989.tb01607.x

[26] Fast, R., Schütt, T., Toft, N., Møller, A., & Berendt, M. (2013). An observational study with long-term follow-up of canine cognitive dysfunction: clinical characteristics, survival, and risk factors. *Journal of veterinary internal medicine, 27*(4), 822–829. https://doi.org/10.1111/jvim.12109

[27] Vite, C. H., & Head, E. (2014). Aging in the canine and feline brain. *The Veterinary clinics of North America. Small animal practice, 44*(6), 1113–1129. https://doi.org/10.1016/j.cvsm.2014.07.008

[28] Prpar Mihevc, S., & Majdič, G. (2019). Canine Cognitive Dysfunction and Alzheimer's Disease - Two Facets of the Same Disease?. *Frontiers in neuroscience, 13*, 604. https://doi.org/10.3389/fnins.2019.00604

[29] Fahnestock, M., Marchese, M., Head, E., Pop, V., Michalski, B., Milgram, W. N., & Cotman, C. W. (2012). BDNF increases with behavioral enrichment and an antioxidant diet in the aged dog. *Neurobiology of aging, 33*(3), 546–554. https://doi.org/10.1016/j.neurobiolaging.2010.03.019

[30] Pan, Y., Landsberg, G., Mougeot, I., Kelly, S., Xu, H., Bhatnagar, S., Gardner, C. L., & Milgram, N. W. (2018). Efficacy of a Therapeutic Diet on Dogs With Signs of Cognitive Dysfunction Syndrome (CDS): A Prospective Double Blinded Placebo Controlled Clinical Study. *Frontiers in nutrition, 5*, 127. https://doi.org/10.3389/fnut.2018.00127

[31] Dowling, A. L., & Head, E. (2012). Antioxidants in the canine model of human aging. *Biochimica et biophysica acta, 1822*(5), 685–689. https://doi.org/10.1016/j.bbadis.2011.09.020

[32] Association for Pet Obesity Prevention. (n.d.). *Association for Pet Obesity Prevention.* https://petobesityprevention.org/

[33] Association for Pet Obesity Prevention. (n.d.). *Pet Caloric Needs.* https://petobesityprevention.org/pet-caloric-needs/

[34] Laflamme D. P. (2005). Nutrition for aging cats and dogs and the importance of body condition. *The Veterinary clinics of North America. Small animal practice, 35*(3), 713–742. https://doi.org/10.1016/j.cvsm.2004.12.011

[35] Geddes, R. F., Finch, N. C., Syme, H. M., & Elliott, J. (2013). The role of phosphorus in the pathophysiology of chronic kidney disease. *Journal of veterinary emergency and critical care (San Antonio, Tex. : 2001), 23*(2), 122–133. https://doi.org/10.1111/vec.12032

[36] Bartges, Joseph W. "Chronic Kidney Disease in Dogs and Cats." *Veterinary Clinics of North America: Small Animal Practice*, vol. 42, no. 4, 2012, pp. 669–692., doi:10.1016/j.cvsm.2012.04.008.

37 Freeman, L. M., Rush, J. E., & Markwell, P. J. (2006). Effects of dietary modification in dogs with early chronic valvular disease. *Journal of veterinary internal medicine, 20*(5), 1116–1126. https://doi.org/10.1892/0891-6640(2006)20[1116:eodmid]2.0.co;2

38 McCarthy, G., O'Donovan, J., Jones, B., McAllister, H., Seed, M., & Mooney, C. (2007). Randomised double-blind, positive-controlled trial to assess the efficacy of glucosamine/chondroitin sulfate for the treatment of dogs with osteoarthritis. *Veterinary journal (London, England: 1997), 174*(1), 54–61. https://doi.org/10.1016/j.tvjl.2006.02.015

39 Roush, J. K., Dodd, C. E., Fritsch, D. A., Allen, T. A., Jewell, D. E., Schoenherr, W. D., Richardson, D. C., Leventhal, P. S., & Hahn, K. A. (2010). Multicenter veterinary practice assessment of the effects of omega-3 fatty acids on osteoarthritis in dogs. *Journal of the American Veterinary Medical Association, 236*(1), 59–66. https://doi.org/10.2460/javma.236.1.59

40 Canine Arthritis Management. (n.d.). *Available Supplements.* https://caninearthritis.co.uk/managing-arthritis/diet-and-nutrition/available-supplements.

41 Plumb, C. (2015). *Plumb's Veterinary Drug Handbook* (8th Ed.) Wiley-Blackwell. 2015.

42 Rialland, P., Bichot, S., Lussier, B., Moreau, M., Beaudry, F., del Castillo, J. R., Gauvin, D., & Troncy, E. (2013). Effect of a diet enriched with green-lipped mussel on pain behavior and functioning in dogs with clinical osteoarthritis. *Canadian journal of veterinary research = Revue Canadienne de recherche veterinaire, 77*(1), 66–74.

43 Bierer, T. L., & Bui, L. M. (2002). Improvement of arthritic signs in dogs fed green-lipped mussel (Perna canaliculus). *The Journal of nutrition, 132*(6 Suppl 2), 1634S–6S. https://doi.org/10.1093/jn/132.6.1634S

44 Lieberthal, J., Sambamurthy, N., & Scanzello, C. R. (2015). Inflammation in joint injury and post-traumatic osteoarthritis. *Osteoarthritis and cartilage, 23*(11), 1825–1834. https://doi.org/10.1016/j.joca.2015.08.015

45 Lieberthal, J., Sambamurthy, N., & Scanzello, C. R. (2015). Inflammation in joint injury and post-traumatic osteoarthritis. *Osteoarthritis and cartilage, 23*(11), 1825–1834. https://doi.org/10.1016/j.joca.2015.08.015

46 Help 'Em Up Harness. (n.d.). *Choosing the Right Harness.* https://helpemup.com/

47 Dr. Buzby's ToeGrips for Dogs. (n.d.). *Help for Your Slipping Dog.* https://toegrips.com/

48 Villalobos, A., & Kaplan, L. (2017) *Canine and Feline Geriatric Oncology: Honoring the Human-Animal Bond.* John Wiley and Sons.

Made in the USA
Coppell, TX
22 February 2021